YOU'RE IN
BUSINESS!

GET A

SUMMER ADVENTURE

JOB

Ryan Jacobson

Illustrations by Jon Cannell

Lerner Publications Company • Minneapolis

For Eric and Kari, my best friends throughout my first summer adventure job. —R.J.

For Mrs. Stephens, my 6th grade teacher who taught creatively and made learning fun. —J.C.

Lerner Publications Company
A division of Lerner Publishing Group, Inc.
241 First Avenue North
Minneapolis, MN 55401 USA

For reading levels and more information, look up this title at www.lernerbooks.com.

Library of Congress Cataloging-in-Publication Data

Jacobson, Ryan.
    Get a summer adventure job / by Ryan Jacobson ; illustrated by Jon Cannell.
        p.   cm. — (You're in business!)
    Includes index.
    ISBN 978-1-4677-3839-2 (lib. bdg. : alk. paper)
    ISBN 978-1-4677-4758-5 (eBook)
    1. Job hunting—Juvenile literature. 2. Employment interviewing—Juvenile literature. I. Cannell, Jon, illustrator. II. Title.
HF5382.7.J334 2014
650.14—dc23   2013041689

Manufactured in the United States of America
1 - CG - 7/15/14

TABLE OF CONTENTS

EARNING MONEY

CAN BE A THRILL!

Having money is a good thing. It makes it possible for you to see the latest summer blockbuster or enjoy that ice-cold treat on a hot day. But *earning* money? That's the tricky part. You don't have to be sixteen to have a job. Still, that doesn't mean finding one is easy. After all, most of the year you're busy with school. So when summer rolls around, you have a choice to make. Do you want to have fun during your free months? Or do you want to spend your time working hard to get some extra cash?

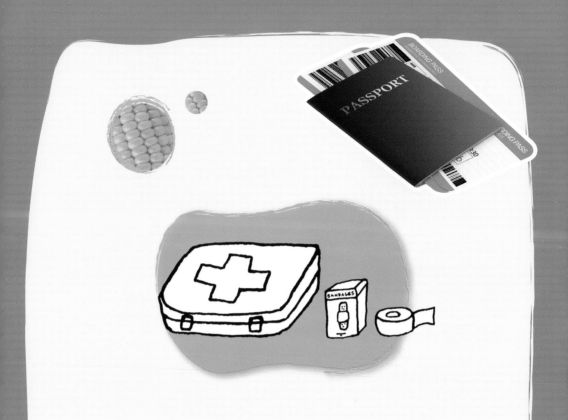

What if you could do both? Well, you can! Plenty of summer jobs can be fun—and even a little thrilling. You can travel, meet new people, try new things, and earn money all at the same time. You'll have so much fun you won't believe you're getting a paycheck! Can you act like a professional? Are you willing to step out of your comfort zone? Then you're ready for a summer adventure job!

JUNIOR CAMP COUNSELOR

What if there was a job that paid you to go camping, play games, practice your hobbies, and spend time with other kids? Believe it or not, there is. You could work as a junior camp counselor and make memories that will last a lifetime—along with some spending money.

A junior camp counselor is an assistant to a camp counselor. You'll help the counselor supervise an assigned group of campers. You may stay in a cabin with the counselor and his or her group. You'll help plan and lead activities, such as games, lessons, and campfire sessions. You'll work behind the scenes from time to time—cleaning the kitchen or mowing the grass, for instance. You may communicate with parents about how their children are doing. You may even work one-on-one with a child who's homesick. Still, this job isn't for everyone. You must enjoy supervising younger children, and it helps to be energetic and outgoing. You must also be patient, caring, and a good role model. Perhaps hardest of all, this summer job usually requires time away from home.

You may spend anywhere from a few nights to several weeks living at the camp. Getting homesick is a real possibility. But if you think you can handle it, and if your family agrees that the job is right for you, opportunity awaits!

If you've attended a summer camp as a camper in the past, you may have a leg up there. But that's not your only option. Do an Internet search to find all the summer camps that are close enough to work at. (How far away is too far? That's up to you and your family.) Most camps do their hiring in March and April. So you should begin your search by February.

The more camps you find, the better your chances of getting a job. But that doesn't mean you should apply everywhere. Read about each camp. Make a list of places that seem like a good match. You'll be spending a lot of time at the camp that employs you. If it doesn't fit your personality or beliefs, your summer could be long and uncomfortable.

Look for camps that focus on activities you enjoy. When you think of summer camp, images of hikes and canoe trips may come to mind. But if you're not especially outdoorsy, never fear. There are also language camps, music camps, acting camps, and sports camps. Find programs that fit your interests.

With your choices narrowed down, see which camps have job openings posted. Check for age restrictions to make sure you qualify. Any camps that advertise positions for junior camp counselors or counselors in training (CITs) should move to the top of your list. But it doesn't hurt to apply at camps that don't list openings. Maybe they're hiring but haven't posted the jobs. Maybe they aren't hiring now but will be soon. If your application is the first or only one to show up, it has a good chance of getting looked at.

The bad news is you could be up against stiff competition. There may be many more applicants than jobs. But there's good news too. If you plan ahead, you can increase your chances of getting the job you want. How? By volunteering!

First and foremost, you need to be good with young kids. Volunteer at a day care center or a children's hospital. Help out with Brownies or Cub Scouts. Co-teach a class at a house of worship. The more you can do, the more impressive your application will be.

You'll also set yourself apart from other applicants by developing your talents. If you're hoping to work at a camp with a specific theme, you'll want to be an expert in that area. A soccer camp will need junior counselors who can play the sport. A Spanish camp will want employees who speak the language.

But don't feel as if you have to zero in on a single hobby just so you can land a job. Potential employers look for people who can pursue and balance a wide range of interests. So if you're musical, learn to play a new instrument. If you like performing, be in the school play. And then go ahead and apply for that job at science camp.

To apply for each job, you'll fill out an application or, better yet, put together a résumé. You should feel good about your chances if you have a long list of experience with children. If you're involved in other activities and get good grades, that'll make your application even better.

With any luck, you'll get called for an interview. Most interviews are conducted face-to-face. But if the camp's far enough away, you may interview over the phone or via computer. Chances are you'll be pretty nervous, and that's okay. Just be yourself and answer the questions as well as you can. With your talents and experience, you can be sure that you're just the type of junior camp counselor they're looking for.

Working Wisdom: Job Applications

Applying for jobs can be a chore. But if you become an expert at filling out applications, you'll fly through the process—and increase your chances of getting hired. To top off your application, get three to five strong references. Start with any adults you've volunteered for. Teachers, coaches, and other instructors are also good options. Always ask permission before listing someone as a reference. Explain the jobs you're applying for, and say why you'd appreciate a recommendation. When you finish those applications, check them over. Be sure that they're neat, easy to read, and mistake-free. Then send them off, and wait and see what happens!

FARMWORKER

Being a junior camp counselor isn't for everyone. But what if you still want to work outdoors—and perhaps spend a summer away from home? Then you may be right for a different kind of adventure job: farmwork.

Whether you live in the heart of farm country or the center of a big city, it's possible to find work on a farm. Some farms offer youth programs that allow kids to live there for part or all of the summer. Farms come in all sizes and types. Small, family-owned farms usually grow a few different crops and have several kinds of animals. Working on this kind of farm is generally the best bet for someone your age.

To work on a farm, you have to get written permission from a parent or a guardian. So your first step is to talk it over with your family. Consider what the experience will be like. If you plan to live on the farm, do you think you can handle being away from home? On the flip side, if you won't live there, how will you get to and from work? Make sure you have a plan for transportation.

Also, think hard about the work itself. Legal farmwork for people under sixteen doesn't involve any unsafe tasks or unreasonable hours. But farming is still tough and physical. Even so, it can also be very rewarding. You'll play a part in making food for others to eat! Are you up for the challenge?

To find out, do some volunteering. If there's a volunteer-run farm near you, spend time working there. Give neighbors a hand with their gardens. Know someone who owns animals? Offer to help with pet care. If possible, join a club that offers farm-related activities, such as 4-H.

If you and your family decide that farm labor is a good fit, your next step is to find a farmer who's hiring. If you live in a rural area, contact local farmers, letting them know you're looking for work. You can also call your local extension office or county Farm Bureau office. They may be able to help you find job opportunities in your area. Check help wanted ads too.

If you live in an urban area, maybe you have relatives or family friends who live in the country. Explore the possibility of living with them and working on a nearby farm. Otherwise, your family can search the Internet together for opportunities across the country. You can also contact Farm Bureau offices throughout your state or region. They may be able to point you toward a few job openings.

When you do find potential employers, put your best foot forward. The farmers may not have applications for you to fill out, so prepare a résumé ahead of time. List your farming-related activities and skills, including your volunteer work.

If you have the right experience and if you look in the right places, you'll find your farming job eventually. But be aware that some farmwork is illegal for people your age to do. Certain farming tasks are dangerous for someone who isn't a skilled professional. These tasks include operating large equipment (think tractors), handling toxic chemicals, and being near certain animals. Even standing on a ladder higher than 20 feet (6 meters) off the ground is a deal breaker.

Working Wisdom: Résumés

A résumé is a one-page list of your work experience and activities. It should be typed in a clear, professional-looking font. Your name and contact information should be at the top of the page. After that, list the places you've worked or volunteered, along with clubs or organizations you're involved with. Include how long you've participated in each activity. For each entry, add a short summary of what you do, what you've learned, or the skills you use.

Your résumé may change based on what job you're applying for. If you apply for a job at a camp, you'll want to put any experience working with kids at the top of the list. If you want to work at a farm, list your outdoor activities or animal-related experience first. You may not have room to include everything you do. Sometimes you'll leave out a few activities that are least relevant to the job you want.

Make sure that your employer is aware of these rules and will respect them. *Never* try to perform an unsafe task, even under supervision.

That still leaves plenty to do, though. You may pick fruits or vegetables. You may feed animals and clean their living spaces. From shoveling straw and manure to painting fences, you'll find ways to keep busy. Occasionally, you may even get to help out at a local farmers' market. At these weekly or monthly events, farmers bring produce to sell at tables or booths. You can help choose and pack the produce that's destined for the farmers' market. Then you can help set up the booth. If you're good at making change, you may be your farmer's cashier for the day. If you're good at talking to people and know a lot about the items you're selling, you can answer customers' questions, explain why your produce is worth buying, and maybe help close a few sales.

No matter what kinds of work you end up doing, you should have an adult supervisor at all times. Follow adults' instructions. They'll guide you through new chores and make sure you stay safe. They should also make sure you get plenty of breaks to eat, drink water, cool off, and rest.

Always feel free to ask questions. Learn as much as you can about the crops you're growing or the animals you're raising. If you work hard and make the most of the opportunity, it will be a summer you'll never forget.

PERSONAL SHOPPER ...

For many people, shopping is an adventure. There's the challenge of searching for the perfect product and the thrill of finding a good deal. Shopping's even better when you don't have to spend your own money. But what if you actually got paid to shop? How cool would that be?

That's the job description of a professional shopper. Some people are too busy to shop. Others are physically unable. And some just don't like to do it. These people hire personal shoppers to take care of everything from buying groceries to picking up gifts for family and friends.

Can you follow instructions? Can you shop from a list? Can you manage someone else's money? Can you easily get to local stores on a bike, on foot, or by bus? If not, can a family member drive you there on a regular basis? And how much are you able to transport? If a shopping list is short, you may be able to fit everything you buy into a backpack or onto a

Bread
Milk
Eggs
Fruit
Rice
Pasta
Butter
Juice

bike basket. But big shopping trips could mean pulling a wagon or a folding shopping cart full of groceries through the neighborhood—even on the hottest days of summer.

Still interested? Then give it a trial run. Start by shopping for your own family. Keep track of which products you need each week or month. Get a sense of average costs for common household items. Notice what brands give you the best quality for the lowest prices.

Once you've got the basics down, expand your experience beyond your own grocery list. If you have grandparents who live nearby or elderly neighbors, ask if you can be their personal shopper for a few weeks. And there may be charities in your area that provide services for people in need. Get involved with those groups. See if you can help run errands for them.

Ready for the real deal? Get out and promote yourself. You can expect a lot of your customers to be senior citizens. So if you have elderly neighbors, family friends, or grandparents, ask them to recommend you to people they know. Post flyers at community centers. Put blurbs in bulletins for places of worship. And don't forget to advertise at grocery and retail stores. Reluctant shoppers will be sure to notice!

When you do find clients, they may want you to be on call. They'll contact you when they need you. Other clients will schedule you for regular deliveries, asking you to run the same errands every week. Still others may simply e-mail you a list or tell it to you over the phone.

Bring a trusted adult along whenever you go into a client's

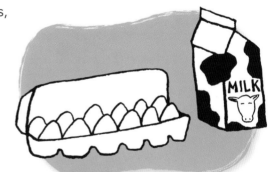

home (unless the client is a grandparent or a close family friend). If you do your shopping alone, let your family know where you'll be and how long you expect to be gone. Always carry a cell phone.

Be sure to get money from your clients in advance. Have them start by giving you the amount of money they expect you to spend on their shopping list. Then, when you return with their items, they'll pay you extra for your services.

Plan your shopping trips wisely, so they take as little time as possible. Follow the list carefully. If a client prefers a certain brand of a product, make sure to get that brand. But if a client is flexible, you have more freedom to look for the best deals. (Generic products are usually cheaper than brand names, and they're often made with the same ingredients or materials.)

Your clients will appreciate your services even more if you can save them money. And that's where the adventure begins. Shopping for good deals is like a treasure hunt. It takes strategy, planning, and some creative thinking. You can even treat it like a game. Challenge yourself to save as much money as possible. With some research and creativity, you'll come up with dozens of money-saving techniques.

Sign up for any free rewards programs that stores offer. Most rewards programs will give you something for free after you spend a certain amount of money. And ask the manager about price matching. If you find something advertised at a lower price somewhere else, the store may be willing to match that price.

Search the Internet for sites that list grocery specials and that compare prices among different stores. Check your local newspapers

for coupons and advertised sales. With your parents' permission, you can also sign up to receive e-mails and special offers from the stores themselves and from various manufacturers.

But never assume that you know what a client will want. Check in before each trip to the store. Mention any coupons or deals you've found to see what sparks interest. Maybe she loves watermelon, but a two-for-one deal may not work for her if she can't eat all that fruit on her own. Or he may not buy ice cream very often, but he may jump at the chance to get a carton at half price. Clearing your plans with your clients ahead of time will prevent you from wasting money on things they don't want—or missing opportunities you weren't expecting.

Save all the receipts from your shopping trips. Give these to your clients along with their groceries. And be sure to return any money that you didn't spend. With each delivery, your clients will see how much money you're saving them. And they'll be more likely to brag about you to their friends, which may get you more paying customers.

NEWSPAPER DELIVERY PERSON

Whether it's every morning, every week, or only once in a while, you may find a newspaper outside your home. Of course, the paper doesn't magically appear. Someone gets paid to put it there: a newspaper delivery person.

Newspaper delivery jobs usually pay pretty well. And jobs do open up, as older delivery people move on to those legendary "sixteen and older" jobs. So if you're reliable and like to work outside, this may be the job for you.

Before you start looking for an opening, figure out if the work will fit into your schedule. Many delivery people must start working very early in the morning. And a route may take several hours to finish. That may not be a problem in the summer, but what if you decide to keep this job when school starts? Will you finish in time to get to school before class begins? Or can you work only on weekends?

If you take a job delivering newspapers every Saturday, you will have to be available every Saturday. It doesn't matter if it's a holiday or if the weather's bad. You'll be expected to work. (On rare occasions, such as a family vacation, you may be able to make other arrangements.)

If you're game to give newspaper delivery a try, keep your eyes peeled for a position. Start by making a list of any newspapers or newsletters that people in your area read. These could be community newsletters, the local paper, or even larger newspapers brought in from other cities. When your list is ready, contact those businesses. Find out if any are looking for delivery people, and ask how you can apply. Even if they aren't hiring, see if you can put in an application or résumé. That way, they'll have your information on file in case something opens up. Then contact them every six months, just to make sure your application isn't forgotten.

Sooner or later, an opportunity will come around. If you can prove that you're hardworking, dedicated, and responsible, you may soon be delivering papers!

Before you start working, find out how many newspapers you'll be expected to deliver. You'll have a specific route assigned to you. Walk or bike along that route ahead of time. See how long it takes you from start to finish. Will you be able to travel that far with a wagon or a backpack full of newspapers? If not, is a family member willing to help you? Work out these details in advance. That'll make your first day on the job less stressful.

At a certain time of day, you'll go to a specific location, called a drop spot. This is where you pick up all the newspapers to deliver. From there, follow the delivery route assigned to you. That probably means pulling your own wagon full of newspapers or riding your bike along the route, carrying the newspapers in a knapsack. Chances are you'll start working before sunrise. Carry a flashlight or have a light on your bike. It's also smart to wear light-colored or reflective clothing. That will make you more visible to drivers.

Drop off a newspaper at every home that's supposed to get one. It sounds pretty basic, but every day can bring new adventures—and challenges. Going near or onto a person's property can be tricky. Some customers may come out and complain that they're not getting their paper early enough or that they don't like where you're leaving it. Be polite and promise to do your best. (But don't be unrealistic. If you can't get there any earlier, don't say you will.) Keep a lookout for dogs that have gotten loose. And of course, at every home that has a pet, watch where you step in the yard!

Because the job can be unpredictable, you should always bring a cell phone with you. Depending on the weather and time of day, you may need sunscreen, a jacket, or an umbrella. Get a good night's sleep on the night before a delivery day. That way, when you finish your route, you'll still have plenty of energy to enjoy the rest of your day!

SUMMER THEATER ACTOR

You can probably name your favorite actors. Maybe you wish you could be more like them. Well, you can! If you enjoy performing, you may be able to get a paying job in summer theater.

This isn't the easiest work to find. Lots of people want it, and few get it. But if you have the talent, the training, and the experience, you could be among the lucky few.

Your first mission is to develop your skills. Discuss your options with a parent or a guardian. Can you enroll in a nearby acting class? What about singing or dance lessons? These almost always cost money, so find out what your family can afford.

There are plenty of other ways to improve your skills— especially the most important skill. You need to be comfortable standing onstage in front of a crowd. So get out there and perform. Join a band, a choir, or a speech team. And of course, try out for parts in every theater production you can find, whether it's a school play or a community event.

Look for volunteer opportunities too. Perhaps your place of worship needs a soloist. Maybe a group is presenting skits at elementary schools or nursing homes. Each chance to perform is a chance to learn something new.

Eventually, you'll feel ready to leap into the theater business. That's when the really hard work begins. First, you need to pinpoint your opportunities. Be prepared: There won't be many. Make a list of the stage theaters near you. Check their websites often, and find out when auditions are held. You and your family can also contact the theaters and request this information. With help from a parent or a guardian, keep an eye on newspapers and theater-related websites. You may discover a call for open auditions.

When an audition is announced in an audition notice, the ad should tell you what to expect and how to prepare. Often you'll be required to send a high-quality photograph (or headshot) of yourself and a résumé. You'll need to memorize and perform a scene or two from a play or a movie. You may also be asked to sing a song.

Auditions aren't as scary as they sound. Real auditions aren't like the ones you see on TV. No one is going to laugh or say mean things to you. Being nervous is okay, but there's no reason to be *really* afraid!

If you do get the role, you're in for a great experience. But there's a lot of work to do. You have to memorize your lines and learn your cues for when to come on- and offstage. There may be dance routines and songs to learn.

That means rehearsals—lots of them. This is a job, so make a good impression by showing up to every rehearsal, being on time, and coming prepared. If you're given a scene to memorize by a certain date, do it. Be aware that rehearsals can last several hours. So pack a lunch or some snacks. And bring something to do while you're waiting to rehearse your next scene. Your parents probably won't be there, so it's up to you to stay occupied and out of trouble!

Like most workers, actors are given paychecks. So with a parent or a guardian's help, open a bank account. You may not get paid a lot of money, but you'll have a great time earning it.

Working Wisdom: Bank Accounts

Once you start making money, you'll want a safe place to keep it. Bank accounts are a lot safer than piggy banks—and can hold a lot more cash. To open a bank account, visit a local bank with a parent or a guardian. The account will probably be in both your names, so you'll both be able to deposit and withdraw money. When you receive a check from an employer, go to the bank, sign the back of the check, and give it to a bank teller to deposit in your account. Or you and your employer can set up a direct deposit system. That way, your money will go straight to your account. Keep your account number written down in a safe place where no one else will find it. You'll be able to check your account online to see how much money you've got. Your parent or guardian will be able to check this info too. When you want to take money out of the account, always make sure to get permission first. Then fill out a withdrawal slip at the bank.

FAMILY HELPER

Are you a champion babysitter? Or maybe you've spent a lot of time doing volunteer work with kids. If you want a summer job that lets you take your skills to a whole new level, put "family helper" at the top of your list.

A family helper is like a super-babysitter. Instead of watching kids from several different families once in a while, you'll work for one specific family for an extended period of time. Being a family helper is a bigger commitment than being a babysitter—but it's also more of an adventure!

Summertime is the perfect season to look for work as a family helper. You've got time on your hands—and a lot of parents don't. During the school year, you may squeeze in a few hours of babysitting on the weekends or during the evenings. But over the summer, you can sub in for a parent anytime! That doesn't mean you should be working all day, every day. But spending a few hours of each weekday with a particular family could give a parent a chance to attend a class or run errands. And it could give *you* an opportunity for some excitement.

What's so exciting about taking care of young kids? The answer's up to you. Learn about the kids' interests. Then find unexpected ways to explore those interests with them. Do they love digging in the dirt? Start a garden in the backyard or in window boxes. Are they big fans of snack time? Help them make their own summer treats from scratch.

Also, introduce kids to new experiences. Go on a photo safari with disposable cameras around the home or the yard. Help the kids put on a play or a talent show. Use a bedsheet to turn a room into a fort, a campsite, or a theater. If your employers are comfortable having you supervise the kids outside the home, head to a nearby library, park, or museum. (Or have employers drop you off at the beginning of your sitting session and pick you up on their way home.) Parents should cover all activity expenses, so check with them before you spend money on anything. Once you have their thumbs-up, let your imagination—and the kids' imaginations—take it from there.

For many families, summer means vacations. Some of your clients may be going on trips. Of course, you may not know anybody who's jetting off to Rome for a month. But you may work for a family that plans to spend a week at a cabin or a beach. Parents who bring young children on family vacations tend to want a little time for themselves, without child care responsibilities. That's where you come in.

If a family you know and trust is going on vacation, offer to come along to help with the kids. Your services will be cheaper than those of a hotel babysitting service or a professional travel nanny. But your clients will still have to pay for your travel expenses, including food and possibly a hotel room. Finding a family that can afford to do this—and one that *your* family is comfortable letting you travel with—may be tough. So if a good opportunity comes along, grab it with both hands!

First, get permission to take your family-helper gig on the road. Then arrange for your family to talk to your potential employers. Make sure your employers agree to cover your travel expenses. They should also agree that you'll be working only a few hours per day. If everyone feels comfortable with the situation, do a contact-info swap and seal the deal. Your employers should also share all the information about their travel plans so that your family can keep tabs on you.

Your journey will likely begin with a road trip or airplane flight. You may need to soothe nervous kids, especially on a plane. (With the parents' permission, keep some hard candy in your pocket for kids to suck during takeoff and landing. This can keep their eardrums from popping.) Be prepared to stave off homesickness and boredom. Brainstorm easily portable games and activities that will fit in a small bag. Depending on the kids' ages and interests, good bets may include small coloring books, trivia cards, and books that you can read out loud. Ask the parents to pack these items or to pay you back for anything you buy for the kids on your own. During the trip, keep an eye peeled to make sure the kids don't lose anything.

Working Wisdom: Safety First

Whenever you're working without adult supervision, keep a cell phone handy. Know your employers' contact information, plus the info for emergency contacts in case your employers can't be reached. Always get an employer's permission before going somewhere unsupervised. If your work takes you outdoors for more than a few minutes at a time, sunscreen is a must. It's also wise to carry Band-Aids and antiseptic cream in case of accidents.

You may also be in charge of supervising bathroom breaks, handling snack time, and wrapping up an activity if it becomes disruptive. Focus on keeping the kids safe and busy. You'll be at your destination before you know it!

Even a trip to the most exciting location won't be all fun and games for you. During your work hours, the kids come first. If that means sticking to the shallow end of the pool when you'd rather be cannonballing off the diving board, make the best of it. Never act bored. Throw all your energy into making sure the kids are having fun. And if you come across an activity you'd like to try for yourself, a place you'd like to explore on your own, or even a great photo op, mentally bookmark it. You can come back later, when you're off duty.

You may not get a chance to vacation with a family. But whether you're on the other side of the country or just in your employers' living room, creativity and a sense of fun can guarantee an unforgettable summer.

PHOTOGRAPHER'S ASSISTANT

Making memories is what summer's all about. And capturing those memories through pictures is probably second nature to you. But photography is also an art—and a job. If you have a good eye for detail and love to get creative, you could spend your summer working as a photographer's assistant.

As a photographer's assistant, you'll pack and carry equipment, help with setup, prepare lighting, and position objects or models to be photographed. You may even be asked to take pictures from a different angle while the photographer snaps shots from his or her spot.

If you want to pursue this job, you'll need a nice camera. Your family may already own one. If not, you'll have to invest in a new camera. Start saving your allowance and any gift money that you receive. You may also need to borrow some money from a relative. Of course, before you do, have a plan for paying it back.

Next, build your skills. Can you enroll in a photography class in your area? If you can't find or afford a class, see if there's a professional photographer—or a photography teacher at a local high school—who will teach you the basics. It may cost a little, but the investment will pay off. A free alternative is to do your own research. Read books, watch videos, and see what tips and tricks you can pick up.

Then start taking pictures. One day, you may focus on flowers. Another day may be about indoor objects. And the day after that you might photograph willing friends and family members. Try different shots from different angles, and find out what gets the best results. Learn how to take pictures inside and outside, at different times of the day, and in different levels of light. Get both close-ups and distance shots under your belt. Experiment with color as well as black and white. Most important, discover what kinds of pictures you most enjoy taking.

You can also look for volunteer opportunities to take pictures. Does your school newspaper need someone to capture shots of sporting events and performances? Is your town holding a special celebration that you could photograph? Does your place of worship need photos for its website? Ask around, and see where your photography skills may be appreciated.

The artistic pictures and the volunteer photos you take are going to come in handy for one

Working Wisdom: Paying Your Debts

Many jobs require some equipment or training that costs money. Your allowance may not be enough to cover those expenses. In that case, you'll need to borrow money from family members or other trusted adults. Figure out how much money you need. Then you and your lender (the person giving you the money) can come up with a plan for paying back that money. You'll probably pay a small amount each month until you reach the total. Once you start making money at your new job, that shouldn't be a problem!

important reason: a photographer's assistant needs a portfolio. That's a small, professional-looking booklet that shows off photos you've taken. The portfolio can be a printed book, a scrapbook, a binder, or a folder. It's what's inside that really matters, though. Your portfolio highlights your experience, talent, and interest in photography.

Put only your best work in a portfolio. You want to show off your skills. You also want to make it clear that you know the difference between a good photo and a not-so-good one.

Once you have your portfolio, you need to find a photographer who wants an assistant—and can afford to pay one. Start by looking up photographers in your area. Introduce yourself and let them know you're looking for work. Offer to let them see your portfolio if they're interested.

You may not find an opportunity right away, but you're getting your name out there. And a few photographers may start thinking about how nice an assistant would be. One of them may eventually call you.

Once you're hired, you may work on projects ranging from senior pictures to family portraits to weddings. When you go to an event offsite, dress as if you're a guest. Be polite and friendly to all the people you see, whether or not they're your clients. Make sure you have permission to take someone's picture before you start snapping photos. Act like a professional, and follow the photographer's directions. You could be well on your way to launching your own career in photography!

GOLF CADDY

•••

Do you know what a hole-in-one is? How about a fairway? What's the difference between an eagle and a bogey? Can you define an albatross? If you understand these terms, then you're probably familiar with the sport of golf. So you may be able to work as a golf caddy.

Of course, the job isn't just about fancy words. A golf caddy carries a bag of clubs from hole to hole while a golfer plays. On top of that, a caddy basically works as a golfer's assistant. You find lost balls. You replace divots—holes left in the ground by clubs. You rake sand traps. You clean the clubs. Most important, a good caddy should be able to offer advice during a round of golf. This includes everything from how far away the hole is and which direction the wind is blowing to suggestions about which club to use for a shot.

You'll need to know the game very well. And there are two ways to learn about golf: by studying the sport and by playing it. Read the rules. Learn the common terms that golfers use. And brush up on

Working Wisdom: Interview like a Pro

The rules for an interview are simple. Dress nicely. Show up on time or a few minutes early. Be polite, but be yourself. You want to show the interviewer that you're qualified for the job. But you also need to be honest. If the interviewer asks about something you don't know how to do, don't lie and say you can do it. Instead, say that you're a fast learner, and focus on what you *can* do. Show the interviewer that you have what it takes to learn on the job and roll with the punches. At the end of the interview, thank the interviewer for his or her time. Follow up with a handwritten or e-mailed thank-you note. Even if you don't get hired, this will make a good impression. You may get a call the next time there's an opening.

golf's etiquette, or unwritten rules. For instance, when you're near a hole, you're never supposed to walk between the ball and the hole!

If you're going to be a caddy, it helps to play the course where you'll be most likely to work. Get to know every golf club and every hole. If you can, play at other golf courses once in a while too. The more knowledge you have, the better advice you'll be able to give and the more desirable a caddy you'll be.

To find potential employers, start by calling the golf courses in your area. Ask how to apply for a caddy job. You'll probably have to fill out an application or drop off a résumé. Later, you may be called in for an interview.

Then search for individual golfers who may want to hire you. That doesn't mean you should approach people at the golf course directly. But if you know any golfers, tell them that you're looking for work. Ask them to tell their golfing friends. With permission and help from a parent or a guardian, you may even post advertisements offering your services. That can mean an announcement on Facebook or flyers hung up around town.

When your opportunity arrives, your main job is to keep your golfer happy. You're not just there to carry the clubs. You're there to offer moral support. Every golfer is different, though. If you talk too much— or not enough—the golfer may not want you next time. Follow the golfer's lead. If he talks a lot, it's okay to do the same. If she's quiet, keep more to yourself. Either way, you should always compliment a

good shot. But don't offer advice unless you're asked, at least at first. Later on, if you get the sense that the golfer wants your input, jump in when he or she seems unsure about something.

You can expect to be paid per round of golf that you work. As you gain more experience and improve your skills, you'll earn even more. Who knows? Someday, you may become a caddy for a professional golfer!

PARTING WORDS

When summer rolls around, you'll have plenty of options for earning money. If you want to try something bold and unusual, those months of work could turn into a once-in-a-lifetime experience. Be ready to work hard. Keep your mind open to the possibilities. Soon you'll be off on a moneymaking adventure!

$$$

NOW WHAT?

If you're ready to start earning money, begin with an action plan. Grab a sheet of paper or hop onto a computer. Then answer the questions below:

Are you comfortable being away from home? For how long? How far away are you willing and able to travel? Do you have a plan for emergencies?

How will you get the training and experience you need? What classes, school-related activities, or volunteer opportunities are available? Who will be your references?

How will you find the job openings in your area? What steps will you need to take to apply for a position?

What are your goals? How much do you hope to earn over the summer?

What kind of help will you need from adults, including your family? Will you need transportation to and from work? Will you need help setting up a bank account? What kind of adult supervision should you expect while you're on the job?

Will you need to file a tax return? By federal law, you must file a tax return if you earn more than a certain amount of money per year. Have an adult help you check IRS Publication 929 to find out what to do.

Will you want to keep your job after the summer is over? If so, can you fit it into your schedule during the school year?

audition: a short performance that shows off a person's skills

comfort zone: a set of situations or routines that are familiar and comfortable, creating a sense of safety

etiquette: the behavior that's expected in a certain situation or environment

investment: spending money on something that will save or earn you more money later

reference: a person who agrees to recommend you to potential employers

résumé: a formal document created for employers that lists a person's education, work history, and skills

Career Kids
http://www.careerkids.com/resume.html
Fill out the simple form at this site, and use it as a starting point for creating your résumé.

Donovan, Sandy. *Job Smarts: How to Find Work or Start a Business, Manage Earnings, and More.* Minneapolis: Twenty-First Century Books, 2012. Learn how to find and succeed in the right kind of job for you.

Fradin, Dennis B., and Judith Bloom Fradin. *Earning.* New York: Marshall Cavendish Benchmark, 2011. This book is a great introduction to working and saving money.

Harmon, Daniel E. *First Job Smarts.* New York: Rosen Publishing, 2010. Learn how to prepare yourself for starting your first job.

It's My Life: Making Money
http://pbskids.org/itsmylife/money/making/index.html
This PBS website offers tips for figuring out what jobs are good fits for you.

Teaching Kids Business
http://www.teachingkidsbusiness.com
Visit this page for a program that will help you prepare to earn and manage your money.

TeensHealth
http://kidshealth.org/teen/school_jobs/jobs/tips_interview.html
Find tips on how to ace a job interview.

Youth Rules!
http://www.youthrules.dol.gov
Check out the Department of Labor's website for the dos and don'ts of working before you're sixteen.

INDEX

PHOTO ACKNOWLEDGMENTS

The images in this book are used with the permission of:
© iStockphoto.com/IngredientsPhoto, p. 2, 32, 35 (golf ball); © Paul Prescott/Shutterstock.com, p. 2, 32, 35 (golf tees); © iStockphoto.com/nito100, p. 3; © Elena Elisseva/Shutterstock.com, p. 4; © Brenda Carson/Shutterstock.com, p. 5; © Zerbor/Shutterstock.com, p. 6 (tree); © Cathleen A. Clapper/Shutterstock.com, p. 6 (marshmallow); © Feng Yu/Shutterstock.com, p. 7; © Olga Lipatova/Shutterstock.com, p. 7, 24, 25, 27; © Diana Taliun/Shutterstock.com, p. 8; © Cathleen A. Clapper/Shutterstock.com, p. 9; © Larry Korb/Shutterstock.com, p. 10; © Maks Narodenko/Shutterstock.com, p. 11; © Elena Schweitzer/Shutterstock.com, p. 13; © Kunal Mehta/Shutterstock.com, p. 14 (grocery store); © Hayati Kayhan/Shutterstock.com, p. 14 (list); © tarasov/Shutterstock.com, p. 17; © magicoven/Shutterstock.com, p. 18; © RTimages/Shutterstock.com, p. 19; © Mammut Vision/Shutterstock.com, p. 21; © iStockphoto.com/nito100, p. 24 (sandcastle); © photosync/Shutterstock.com, p. 24 (backpack); © Andrii Groulko/Shutterstock.com, p. 26; © iStockphoto.com/cloki, p. 27 (bandaid); © schankz/Shutterstock.com, p. 28 (film strip, top); © Pavel Isupov/Shutterstock.com, p. 28 (roll of film, bottom); © Jarp2/Shutterstock.com, p. 30; © Vadim Georgiev/Shutterstock.com, p. 31 (photos).

Front Cover: © Paul Prescott/Shutterstock.com, (golf tees); © Elena Elisseva/Shutterstock.com, (marshmallows); © Skylines/Shutterstock.com, (camera); © iStockphoto.com/IngredientsPhoto, (golf balls).

Main body text set in Avenir LT Std 11/18.
Typeface provided by Adobe Systems.